PIANO

MAKING ♪ MUSIC
KATE RIGGS

CREATIVE 🍎 EDUCATION

PUBLISHED *by* Creative Education
P.O. Box 227, Mankato, Minnesota 56002
Creative Education is an imprint of The Creative Company
www.thecreativecompany.us

DESIGN AND PRODUCTION *by* Ellen Huber
ART DIRECTION *by* Rita Marshall
PRINTED *in the* United States of America

PHOTOGRAPHS *by*
Corbis (Andersen-Ross, Hill Street Studios/Blend Images,
Stanislas Merlin/cultura), Getty Images (Clarissa Leahy, Jan
Ruckers, WireImage), iStockphoto (Don Bayley, iLexx, Ela
Kwasniewski, David H. Lewis, Yulia Saponova), Shutterstock
(Africa Studio, Aschindl, Linda Bucklin, Asaf Eliason,
GSPhotography, J. Helgason, Krasowit, Ela Kwasniewski,
kwest, Jill Lang, luchschen, Luminis, Mark McClare,
Photoseeker, Popova Valeriya, Vorobyeva, Hank Vrieselaar)

LIBRARY OF CONGRESS
CATALOGING-IN-PUBLICATION DATA
Riggs, Kate.
Piano / Kate Riggs.
p. cm. — (Making music)
SUMMARY: *A primary prelude to the piano, including what
the keyboard instrument looks and sounds like, basic instructions
on how to play it, and the kinds of music that feature it.*
Includes bibliographical references and index.

ISBN 978-1-60818-369-2
1. Piano—Juvenile literature. 1. Title.

ML650.R54 2013
786.2—DC23   2013009498

FIRST EDITION
9 8 7 6 5 4 3 2 1

TABLE OF CONTENTS

WHEN YOU HEAR A PIANO

Water flowing in a stream.

A cat pouncing on a mouse.

Stars twinkling in the sky.

What do you think of when you hear a piano?

Water rushes over rocks.
A cat creeps up behind a mouse.

THE KEYBOARD FAMILY

Musical instruments that sound and look alike belong

to a "family." Pianos belong to the keyboard family.

Keyboards have a set of keys that are pressed

down with fingers to make sounds. Pianos are also

stringed instruments whose strings are hidden.

The keyboard family has included many different instruments over the centuries.

accordion

electronic keyboard

pump organ

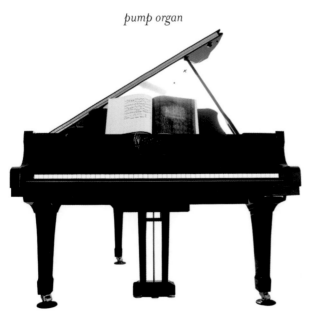

grand piano

pipe organ

Grand pianos have flat frames, and the strings stretch sideways.

PARTS OF A PIANO

A piano's strings are inside a wooden frame.

Pianos have keyboards that are attached to the strings.

You press a key to make the string **vibrate**.

A part called a hammer hits the string and bounces off.

When you press down hard on a key, the hammer

hits the string hard. This makes a loud sound.

An upright piano's strings are vertical, but the hammers run sideways.

MAKING MUSIC

PIANO KEYS AND PEDALS

There are 88 keys on a piano keyboard. Fifty-two of

the keys are white. The other keys are shorter and black.

A piano has two or three **pedals** near the floor.

A pianist presses a pedal with his or her foot to make

the notes last longer or sound softer.

Mainly American-made pianos have all three pedals.

Black keys used to be made from a wood called ebony.

The concert grand piano makes a beautiful, singing sound.

KINDS OF PIANOS

There are many kinds of pianos.

Many upright pianos are 40 to 52 inches (102–132 cm)

tall and about 58 inches (147 cm) wide.

Grand pianos can be four to nine feet (1.2–2.7 m) across.

Concert grand pianos are the largest pianos.

upright piano

MAKING MUSIC

PLAYING THE PIANO

You sit on a bench in front of the piano keyboard.

Your arms are straight in front of you. Your

fingers are curved and pointing down toward the keys.

Use your fingers to press on the keys and play!

Press down three or more keys at a time
to play a chord, or a group of notes.

A pianist practices
for a long time before
he plays for others.

A harpsichord's strings are plucked instead of hammered.

ACTA
VIRVM
PROBANT · 1654 ·

EARLY PIANOS

The first pianos were made in the 1700s.

They were called pianofortes (*pee-AN-oh-FOR-tayz*),

a word that means "soft-loud." They were different

from earlier keyboard instruments like harpsichords

(*HARP-sih-kordz*). The player could play softly and

loudly on the pianoforte.

Harpsichords have only one **volume**.

harpsichord

PIANO MUSIC

Pianists play every kind of music.

They play with groups of musicians or alone.

Two people can sit at the

same piano and play duets.

People can learn to play piano when they are young or old.

Two people playing on the same piano is also called piano four-hands.

A pianist who plays with a choir is called an accompanist.

A PIANIST PLAYS

A pianist sits down at a piano bench.

Her hands flow across the keys.

A **choir** sings along

to the piano's soulful sound!

Elton John sang and played at a 2012 concert in Sydney, Australia.

Elton John was born in England in 1947.

He loved to sing and play piano from a young age.

Elton joined his first band in 1965.

He has been playing music at concerts around the world

since 1969. He has written music for hundreds

of songs and **recorded** *many albums.*

Elton often sings and plays piano at the same time.

GLOSSARY

choir: *a group of people who sing together*

pedals: *foot-operated levers at the base of a piano*

recorded: *made a CD or tape of something that can be played later*

vibrate: *to shake or move up and down rapidly*

volume: *the loudness or softness of a sound*

READ MORE

Ganeri, Anita. *Pianos and Keyboards.*
North Mankato, Minn.: Smart Apple Media, 2012.

Levine, Robert. *The Story of the Orchestra.*
New York: Black Dog & Leventhal, 2001.

Storey, Rita. *The Piano and Other Keyboard Instruments.*
North Mankato, Minn.: Smart Apple Media, 2010.

WEBSITES

Activity TV: Make a Thumb Piano
http://www.activitytv.com/779-make-thumb-piano
Watch the video to learn how to make a tiny piano!

San Francisco Orchestra Kids Music Lab
http:www.sfskids.org/templates/musicLabF.asp?pageid=14
Use this keyboard to play fun songs!

Every effort has been made to ensure that these sites are suitable for children, that they have educational value, and that they contain no inappropriate material. However, because of the nature of the Internet, it is impossible to guarantee that these sites will remain active indefinitely or that their contents will not be altered.